Ballet for Boys and Girls

Ballet for

Illustrated with photographs by Costas, and others

Boys and Girls

Kathrine Sorley Walker & Joan Butler

PRENTICE-HALL INC., *Englewood Cliffs, New Jersey*

Printed in the United States of America   J
Prentice-Hall International, Inc., London
Prentice-Hall of Australia, Pty. Ltd., North Sydney
Prentice-Hall of Canada, Ltd., Toronto
Prentice-Hall of India Private Ltd., New Delhi
Prentice-Hall of Japan, Inc., Tokyo
Prentice-Hall of Southeast Asia Pty. Ltd., Singapore
Whitehall Books Limited, Wellington, New Zealand

1 2 3 4 5 6 7 8 9 10

Library of Congress Cataloging in Publication Data
Butler, Joan.
  Ballet for boys and girls.
  Bibliography: p. 94
  SUMMARY: Discusses ballet techniques and steps, dancers, companies, costumes, and stories of famous ballets.
  1. Ballet—Juvenile literature. [1. Ballet] I. Walker, Kathrine Sorley, joint author. II. Costas. III. Title.
GV1787.5.B87   792.8   78-27402
ISBN 0-13-055574-6

Ballet for Boys and Girls

Ballet is dancing.
Ballet is movement—fast movement or slow
movement—to music.
Ballet is theater.

This picture of Leslie Roy and Christopher d'Amboise
of the School of American Ballet in Jerome Robbins's *Dances
at a Gathering* shows how exciting and enjoyable ballet can be.

Ballet is a shared activity between boys and girls and
men and women, like skating or mixed doubles in tennis.
The girl contributes neatness, quickness, and grace.
The boy contributes greater muscular strength for jumping
and for lifting the girl high in the air.

These two dancers make it all look easy and fun to do.
But as in all physical activities, before you get to that stage
you have to work very hard.

For those who watch, ballet is full of variety.
It's a good leisure interest, with plenty to learn, think
about, and get enthusiastic about.

or those who take part, ballet is a morning-to-night
all-out occupation.
Just like sports, it takes all they can give of physical,
mental, and emotional power.
Pole-vaulters, gymnasts, or high divers who dedicate
themselves to preparing for the Olympic Games have to be strict
about training.
They have to be careful about diet and sleep and relaxation.
They have to cut out drinking and smoking and listen to
their coaches' advice.
Each one has to concentrate all the time on trying to
achieve, and then to better his or her best performance.

In exactly the same way, ballet dancers work at dancing.
They have to do everything their teachers, and the people
who create the ballets, ask them to do.

allet dancers start very young.
All their lives they have to go regularly to classes.
This picture shows a scene familiar to everyone interested
in ballet:

A large studio, with mirrors on the walls.
A rehearsal pianist at a piano.
A teacher.
Students wearing practice clothes of leotards and tights.

Classes, even for the stars, begin like this one with deep *pliés*
at the *barre*.
The word *plié* is French.
French is the international language of ballet.
When dancers speak of *pliés* they mean bending the knees.
Doing *pliés* warms up the leg muscles for the rest of the exercises.

The *barre* is exactly that. It is a wooden bar fixed around
the walls of the studio about 3 feet 6 inches from the ground.
Dancers hold this *barre* with one hand to help them to balance.
They watch what they are doing in big mirrors on the walls.
In these they can see mistakes and correct them.

At this point in a class dancers wear woolen leg warmers.
This is another way of making sure that the muscles
stay soft and flexible.

*A*ll *the steps* in ballet are based on five basic positions of
the feet.
These have to be learned right from the beginning.
They look like this:

First position	Second position	Third position	Fourth position	Fifth position

To do them properly the legs have to be "turned out" from the hips.
If you try them you will see what this means.

There are five basic positions, too, for the arms.
They look like this:

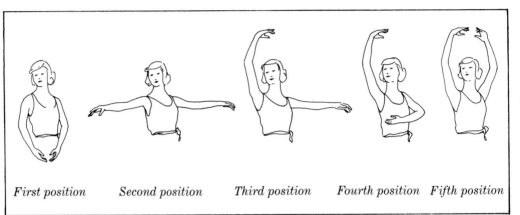

First position *Second position* *Third position* *Fourth position* *Fifth position*

If you check with the diagrams you will see that the junior students in this picture are doing *pliés* with their feet in the second position and their arms in the first position.

Limbering up the back and limbs is every bit as important
in ballet as in all the athletic sports.
Limbering exercises like these demonstrated by Galina Panov
are usually done at the *barre*, before a class begins.

After the work
at the *barre*,
the dancers move
into the center of
the studio for
further exercises.
Dancers have to
learn good balance
and physical control.
Many of the most
famous steps and
positions they
practice date back
almost 200 years.
Among these are
attitudes, which
these boys are
demonstrating.
In an *attitude*,
the free leg is bent
at the knee and
lifted behind to the
level of the hip.

Equally important are *arabesques*.
In an *arabesque*, the free leg is held straight.
In this picture a teacher corrects a junior boy's *arabesque*
so that he balances his body correctly.

Arabesques can be done with the supporting leg straight,
or bent at the knee in *demi-plié* (half-*plié*).
The girl in the foreground of the picture at the top of the opposite
page is looking intently in the mirror to check that she is
in the right position.

The same kind of *arabesque* is repeated onstage by
Jean-Pierre Bonnefous of New York City Ballet in the last act
of the ballet *Coppélia*.

All classroom exercises have a purpose.
They are planned to strengthen the body, to make it
supple, and to give the student greater stamina.
Stamina—being able to go on dancing for a long time
—is very important, as it is in sports.

After the work at the *barre* and the first center exercises,
the dancers practice jumps.
There are many kinds of jumps.
This senior student at the School of American Ballet
demonstrates one called an *échappé sauté*.

Small jumps are a preparation for bigger and higher ones. Jumps in which a dancer leaps off one foot and lands on the other are called *jetés*.

These boys of the Leningrad Kirov Ballet are exciting to watch as they do *jetés* in unison.

17

Onstage, Wayne Eagling of England's Royal Ballet demonstrates a *jeté* in Act III of the ballet *Swan Lake*.

Ballet is not unisex.
It aims at stressing the natural differences in the bodies of men and women.
They have to be trained and developed differently.
Almost from the beginning there will be differences between the exercises for girls and those for boys.
When they begin to dance together as partners, which is called "double, or supported, work," the boy's extra strength is used to display the girl to good advantage.

In this picture, two dancers of the Leningrad Kirov Ballet
practice what is called a "supported *arabesque*."
Although the photograph is taken from another angle,
the woman is in the same position as the dancers
in the pictures on page 15.
This time, however, she is being supported by a partner.

In supported work the woman is not always on the ground. Nowadays in fact she spends a great deal of time onstage being lifted, carried, or thrown from one partner to another.

The most spectacular part of a *pas de deux* (a dance
for two) comes with the high lifts.
Lifts are a collaboration.
Timing, balance, and correct breathing all play a part.
The woman breathes in just at the moment her partner lifts her.
She helps him, too, by pushing off the ground at
the right moment and in the right rhythm.
Once he has lifted her, the man straightens out his arms
and "locks" his elbows to keep her up there. Then he can run
around the stage holding her high above his head.
None of the physical effort should show.
The effect should be one of ease and relaxation, as in
this photograph of dancers at the School of American Ballet.

As with jumps, there are many kinds of high lifts.
Here is another, demonstrated by Kay Mazzo and Peter Martins
of New York City Ballet in George Balanchine's
Stravinsky Violin Concerto.

Think of a young woman's weight, and compare the male dancer's
type of strength, in which you can hardly see the arm
and shoulder muscles at work, with the overdeveloped muscles
that go with "pumping iron."
Of course, weight-lifters' weights don't help on
the way up, as a good partner does!

22

But the same kind of physical strength is needed by
the male dancer.
The muscles develop differently because the training
is different.

Here is another lift, in a Soviet ballet called *Traveling Circus*.
This time it is done for comic effect.
The strong man appears to be having a hard time
holding up the tightrope walker.

One of the most obvious differences between the work of a girl and that of a boy in ballet is that the girl dances on the points of her toes.

This is something she learns when she is about ten years old. She must not do it earlier because her bones are too soft and still growing, and it can seriously hurt the feet, hips, and back if it is begun too soon.

Now she learns how to do on *pointe* all the steps she has already learned, and a great many more.

The special shoes she wears are called "blocked shoes."
The way they are cut out and made up is a specialized craft.
They are graded in strength as well as size.
There are different toe shapes—tapered, medium broad, and square.
The shoes have to fit perfectly.
They are fastened with a drawstring that a dancer adjusts
to her liking, and with the long ribbons that the girl in
the picture on the opposite page is going to tie.

These pictures, of Capezio shoes, show the ribbons and
the drawstring clearly.
The others show various stages of the shoe's construction.

The blocked shoe is simply a support to help the dancer
to stand on her toes.
It doesn't do the work for her.
The feet have to be strengthened with the right exercises
and used in the right way.

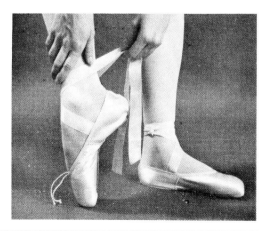
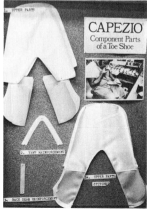
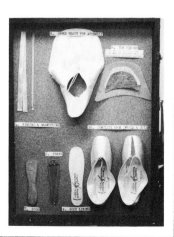

These New York City Ballet dancers in Balanchine's *Concerto Barocco* show the flying effect of a number of girls poised briefly on *pointe*.

In supported work, when the girl is on *pointe*,
she immediately seems lighter, more feminine, and more graceful.
This is certainly true of Judith Fugate of New York City Ballet,
partnered by Daniel Duell in Balanchine's *Valse-Fantaisie*.

Valse-Fantaisie is a romantic ballet, as the pose and
the pretty costume for the girl suggest.
Here is a less romantic view of supported work, shown
by Karin von Aroldingen and Bart Cook in *Stravinsky
Violin Concerto*.

*T*he *high spot* of an old-style ballet like *Coppélia*
comes in the last act.
Then the principal pair of dancers show their skill
in spectacular dances.

These traditional showpieces always have the same form.
There is a *pas de deux*, then solos for the man and the woman, and a
quick (*allegro*) finale, called a coda,
which they dance together.

28

The *pas de deux* is an exhibition of split-second
cooperation between the dancers.
Here Patricia McBride and Peter Martins of
New York City Ballet display the firm balance of the ballerina
and the steady support she is given by her partner.

After the *pas de deux* the man dances an exciting
and vigorous solo, full of virtuoso steps and high jumps.

The woman's solo, on the other hand, is light and
delicate in style.
It has very precise footwork.
Her arms and hands are used softly and gracefully, where
the man's arm movements have been large and sweeping.

Coppélia is a comedy ballet about peasants in central Europe
and the dances have something of a folk dance air.
La Bayadère is pure classical dancing at its finest, as
shown here by Gabriela Komleva and Sergei Vikulov of
the Leningrad Kirov Ballet.

*O*ne of the most exciting of the traditional *pas de deux*
is this one, danced by Antoinette Sibley and Anthony
Dowell of the Royal Ballet.
It is from Act III of *The Sleeping Beauty*.
It is usually called the Aurora *pas de deux*, from the name
of the ballet's heroine, the Princess Aurora.

The very complicated step illustrated in the picture is always a delight to watch. It is called a "fish dive" and the dancers do three in a row. The ballerina does a *pirouette* (a turn), guided by the man's left arm. Then he catches her around the waist. She dives forward, raising her legs into the position in the photograph, balanced on her partner's knee. The whole combination of movements has to be done smoothly and quickly. Above all, it has to look easy.

The traditional *pas de deux* usually represents the fairy tale "happy ending" of a love story. However difficult the steps, it is danced with an appearance of exhilaration and enjoyment.

In male dancing, the aim of jumping is to show strength
and athletic vigor, and to jump as high as possible.
The technical phrase for this is "to have good elevation."
In classical ballet the dancer never turns somersaults during
a jump, as a trampoline performer or a gymnast does. But there
are other, quite complicated, steps and spins that are allowed.
It depends on the height of the jump and the control of
the dancer just how much is possible.
Great Russian dancers like Rudolf Nureyev and Mikhail
Baryshnikov have astonished everyone with their jumps.

When women do jumps the aim is to show speed and lightness.
With both sexes, it is important that they hold
a position correctly while they are in the air.

In dancing, people often talk about "good line."
This means that the outline of the dancer's body, head, and
limbs should be presented correctly to the viewer.

This picture shows the New York City Ballet's *corps de ballet*
jumping forward in unison in *Bournonville Divertissements*.

The way steps in ballet are performed varies according to
what they are supposed to express.
In the previous picture the *corps de ballet* showed youthful energy
and high spirits.
In this picture of Natalia Makarova and Fernando Bujones
in American Ballet Theatre's production of *La Sylphide*,
the jump has another meaning.

The story of *La Sylphide* is a Scottish legend.
    It is about a young man called James who falls in love
with a supernatural creature called a sylphide.
The photograph shows a moment when the Sylphide is supposed
to be visible only to James and not to the other people onstage.
Makarova's beautiful *jeté* gives the impression that she has wings.

The ballet ends sadly.
James listens to a wicked witch who gives him a magic scarf.
The witch tells him that if he wraps this around the
Sylphide's arms she will become human. Instead, she dies.
Meanwhile, he has lost the love of the village girl he meant
to marry.

La Sylphide is a very old ballet.
It was first given at the Paris Opera in 1832 and at that
time it was a novelty.
There was a worldwide interest then in what we might now
describe as Gothic tales.
All the arts—literature, music, painting, drama—went
through what is called the Romantic Era.
The stories were about heroes and heroines and villains, about
madness and betrayal, about spells and revenge.

La Sylphide was one of the
first Romantic ballets.
The ballerina who danced the
leading role was famous
all over Europe.
She was Marie Taglioni.
No photographs were possible
in those days but many
drawings and engravings
of her remain.
This one shows her in
the second act of *La Sylphide*.
The Sylphide offers James
various woodland treasures,
like the bird's nest Taglioni
has in her hand.

Two important factors helped to give the illusion that the ballerina was superhuman.

Taglioni was one of the first ballerinas to wear blocked shoes.
They were not really blocked in the modern sense.
They were simply reinforced at the toe so that she could poise for a second or so.
Nowadays of course a ballerina does most of her dancing on *pointe*.
However, it was then an exciting development that suggested flight.

The other new ideas came from the stage engineers of the time.
They invented theater tricks to make it look as if she were supernatural.
If you go to a performance of *La Sylphide*, look out for two of these.
In the first act there is a wide chimney and inside it is a pulley that is invisible to the audience.
When the ballerina catches at the pulley she is lifted up the chimney very quickly.
In the next act, the woodland, there is a tiny device behind a tree trunk.
When the Sylphide puts her foot on this she is lifted up to the branches to fetch the bird's nest, and then lowered down again.

By the time of *La Sylphide*, ballet had already been happening for a very long while.

It began at the Italian and French courts in the fifteenth century.
Then, dances representing stories were made into entertainments for the rulers and their courtiers.
These were called ballets.

They looked very unlike the ballets we see now.
They were performed in the center of the great palace halls.
The audience sat on tiers on three sides.
The dancers were not professional performers.
They were courtiers themselves and the clothes they wore were
the fashionable court dresses of the time.
Sometimes they wore headdresses that represented the characters
they were playing.

These two dancers of the seventeenth century are wearing the
elaborate and rather heavy dresses of the time.
Note the shoes with heels.

J. Berin del.

Most of the stories were about gods and goddesses, and there
was music and singing as well as dancing.
In a masque, which was a similar kind of entertainment,
there were spoken scenes as well.

Even kings took part.
Louis XIV of France gained his nickname of the Sun King
(Le Roi Soleil) from a role he played in a ballet.

*A*s people became more interested in the dancing and less
in the purely spectacular side of the show, these heavy
dresses were simplified.
No one could do any very interesting steps while wearing them.
Heelless slippers were gradually introduced.
Skirts were shortened too so that the feet and ankles of
the women were more easily seen.
As the dances became more complicated, the courtiers stopped
performing and professional dancers took over.
The French, who were pioneers of dance at this time, established
a national school in Paris, the Académie Royale de la Danse,
in 1661.
Audiences began to have favorite dancers who became great
international stars.
Two of these ballerinas were Marie Sallé, who is shown in
this painting, and Marie-Anne Cupis de Camargo.
Their supporters formed into rival factions.
This kind of rivalry among the fans of famous dancers
has gone on ever since.

$\mathcal{M}$ale dancers were as popular as ballerinas.
Two famous ones were a father and son called Vestris—
Gaetan and Auguste.
Gaetan, the father, was nicknamed the God of the Dance
(Le Dieu de la Danse)—partly in fun, as he thought
very highly of himself.

They were both brilliant dancers, however.
The one in this picture is Auguste.

*R*ivalry *between* ballerinas continued to flourish very strongly in the early nineteenth century.
This was the time of the Romantic ballet and of Marie Taglioni.
But there were many other great dancers.

One of Taglioni's principal rivals was Fanny Elssler, seen here in a very popular Spanish dance, the Cachucha. Elssler visited America in 1840 and was as successful here as she was in Europe. Another rival of Taglioni and Elssler was Carlotta Grisi. The most famous role she created was Giselle, in 1831, and the ballet is still as popular today as it was then. Almost every great ballerina has danced Giselle.
In this photograph Karen Kain and Frank Augustyn of the National Ballet of Canada show how it looks today.

Giselle is another Romantic story, about a peasant girl who goes mad and dies when she finds that her lover is really a prince and engaged to marry a princess.
In the second act, Giselle's ghost leaves the grave to join the Wilis.
These are the spirits of girls who have died for love.
They revenge themselves on men by making them dance until they drop dead.

Long ballets were popular in the nineteenth century. They always had complicated plots with many incidents and characters. *La Esmeralda* (1844) was one of the favorites. It was based on the novel *The Hunchback of Notre Dame* by Victor Hugo. The story is a very dramatic one, about a gypsy girl Esmeralda, with whom the hunchback Quasimodo is in love. *She*, of course, is in love with a poet called Gringoire. This picture shows Carlotta Grisi and Jules Perrot as Esmeralda and Gringoire.

Jules Perrot was one of the most interesting and important *premiers danseurs* (leading male dancers) at this time. He started life as an acrobat and tumbler in a company of entertainers, traveling through the provinces of France. In addition to being a star dancer, he created ballets. The person who does that is called a choreographer. Choreography always seems a mysterious word to the layman. It comes from the Greek and means composing dances—and that is what a choreographer does. Sometimes the dances tell a story, as Perrot's *Esmeralda* did. Often they simply match up with music to make a beautiful or interesting theatrical production.

In the last years of the nineteenth century, a French dancer and choreographer went to work in Russia. He was Marius Petipa, and the theater he worked at became very famous in ballet history. It was the Maryinsky Theatre in St. Petersburg. That was in the time of the tsars, before the Russian Revolution. Now, in Soviet Russia, the same theater is called the Leningrad Kirov. It still houses a great ballet company and its school. One of the ballets the Kirov performs is well known to us all— *Swan Lake.*

Swan Lake with choreography by Marius Petipa and Lev Ivanov was first given in St. Petersburg in 1895. It has a fairy-tale story.

The Swan Princess, Odette, has been put under a spell
by a magician.
The spell can be broken only if a prince promises to marry her.
Prince Siegfried falls in love with her, but the magician
tricks him into promising to marry the magician's own daughter,
Odile, disguised as Odette.

The two roles of Odette and Odile are usually danced by one
ballerina. As their characters are completely different, this is a
test of the ballerina's range of expression.

In this photograph, Alla Osipenko of the Leningrad Kirov
Ballet is dancing Odile with John Markovsky as Prince Siegfried.

The Kirov Ballet dancers are particularly noted for the
excellence of their technique.
The three famous Russian dancers who have made their homes in
the West, Natalia Makarova, Rudolf Nureyev, and Mikhail
Baryshnikov, were all members of the Kirov Ballet.

The other great Soviet ballet company with a long history
is at the Bolshoi Theatre in Moscow.
Marius Petipa's ballets are performed there as well.
The Bolshoi dancers are exciting and theatrical.

This photograph is of Ekaterina Maximova and Vladimir Vassiliev in Petipa's *Don Quixote*.

Another ballet company with a fine tradition, like the Leningrad Kirov and the Bolshoi Ballet, is the Royal Danish Ballet.
It also has a dance style of its own, called after a famous Danish choreographer, August Bournonville.

Bournonville studied at the Paris Opera with Auguste Vestris and loved the Romantic ballet.
In 1836 he staged *La Sylphide* in Copenhagen.

Often, even now, various choreographers use the same musical score and story, if there is one, but compose their own dances and action. For instance, there are many different versions of *Romeo and Juliet* set to the score by Serge Prokofiev.

In Paris, the choreographer of *La Sylphide* was Marie Taglioni's father, Filippo. In Copenhagen, Bournonville composed the choreography.
He even used different music, but the story was the same. Bournonville's version is the one we usually see today.

Bournonville composed many more ballets.
One of the most popular
is *Napoli* (Naples). It is another fairy tale, about Neapolitan fisherfolk and the sea spirits in the Bay of Naples.
These three dancers of the Royal Danish Ballet are performing a *pas de trois* (dance for three) that is typical of the lively and elegant Bournonville style.

In the old story-ballets, the story is told partly by a language of gestures that is called mime.

Some of the gestures make sense only if you know what they mean. For instance, if a dancer raises her arms in the fifth position and moves her hands around each other in the air, that signifies "dancing." Some gestures, however, are very easy to understand. The boy in this picture, one of the child dancers in New York City Ballet's *The Nutcracker*, is pointing to himself, which means "me" or "I." Sometimes only one hand is used.

If the boy then did the "dancing" gesture, this would mean "I am going to dance."

Another gesture easy to understand is the one these young students in England are learning.

If you point to the third finger of your left hand—the "wedding ring" finger—or pretend that you are slipping a wedding ring onto it with the fingers of the right hand, this means marriage.

In most of the older ballets there are one or two roles
that have no real dancing in them. They are acted roles,
and the dancers who do them are sometimes called mimes.

A ballet with an important mime role is *Coppélia*.
The story is about a young village girl, Swanilda, who teases an
old toymaker, Dr. Coppélius, by pretending to be his life-size
doll Coppélia come to life. The mime role is that of Dr. Coppélius.

This picture, of Vanessa Harwood and Constantin Patsalas of
the National Ballet of Canada, shows Swanilda wearing the doll's
dress in Dr. Coppélius's workshop.

Coppélia was first produced in Paris in 1870.
This was at the only time in the history of ballet when
male dancers were less important than ballerinas.
In the court ballet days, men were dominant.
The Sun King and many other noblemen were the most acclaimed
dancers. Men directed the spectacles, designed the elaborate
costumes, composed and performed the music.
When dancing became a profession, men and women were equally
talented and popular as dancers.
Men, however, were usually the teachers.
Men were the choreographers, designers, and composers.

In the time of the Romantic ballet of course the ballerinas were adored.
Taglioni, Elssler, Grisi, and others had countless fans and supporters.
Admirers even drank champagne from their ballet slippers.
All the same, male dancers were equally acclaimed.
There were the two Vestris, Perrot, Marius Petipa and his
brother Lucien, who was first to dance the prince in *Giselle*; and
Arthur Saint-Léon, who later choreographed *Coppélia*.
When *Coppélia* was produced, however, the fashion at the Paris
Opera was for the hero in a ballet to be danced by a young woman.
This spoiled the balance of a ballet very badly.
It meant that there was no interesting supported work.
One dancer was never strong enough to lift another.
It meant too that there was no contrast of masculine vigor, strong
jumps, and turns, with the softer and lighter feminine dances.
The fashion went the way of all fashions. It changed.
When *Coppélia* was produced in Russia some years later
the hero, Franz, was danced by a man.
Now it is always a man's role.
Even when Franz was danced by a young woman, however, the
mime role of Dr. Coppélius was taken by a man.

he old gesture language of mime is rarely used in modern ballets. Instead, when there is a story, the dancers tell it by the way they dance. They express moods through their movements. In *The Moor's Pavane*, as danced by American Ballet Theatre, the story is about Othello, and is an episode from Shakespeare's play. The villain, Iago, asks his wife, Emilia, to steal a precious handkerchief from Othello's wife, Desdemona.

In this picture, Sally Wilson as Emilia shows her happiness at having managed to do this. In the background are Othello, Iago, and Desdemona. The lost handkerchief causes Othello to believe that Desdemona is unfaithful to him and he strangles her. When he discovers that she was innocent, he kills himself.

When choreographers compose ballets, they cannot do it at home with pen and paper, as musicians can compose music or writers write books.

They have to work in the studio with dancers.

They listen to music that they have chosen.

They are dancers themselves so they can "see" in their mind's eye some steps that they think will suit the music.

Then they describe the steps to a dancer.

From the way the dancer performs them, the choreographer will get ideas for the rest of the dance.

In this picture Arthur Mitchell of the Dance Theatre of Harlem is beginning a new ballet and demonstrating a step to one of the ballerinas, Virginia Johnson.

55

Most classical ballet choreographers
are men but a few are women.
Marie Taglioni was one of the first
women to choreograph a ballet.
She choreographed only one, *Le Papillon*
(The Butterfly).

In this picture one of today's
women choreographers, Lynn Seymour,
is working on her ballet
The Court of Love, with dancers
of the Sadler's Wells Royal Ballet.

One type of job in classical ballet has been supremely well
done by women. The key person at the head of a ballet company
is usually the artistic director. An artistic director is not
a dictator. Other people offer advice about which ballets
should be staged and which dancers should dance them.
The artistic director has to collaborate, too, with the people who
look after money matters. All the same, an artistic director
is largely responsible for what we see on the stage, and many of
the best have been, or are, women. Marcia Haydée, the artistic
director of the Stuttgart Ballet, is also a leading dancer.
This picture shows her with Richard Cragun in John Cranko's
The Taming of the Shrew.

Preserving the choreography of ballets has always been
a problem. It was always difficult to write down dances.
Many people tried—most of the choreographers of the past

invented their own shorthand systems but none of them was
completely satisfactory.
Ballets continued to be handed down from one generation of dancers
to another by word of mouth or demonstration.
Dancers are celebrated for having fantastic memories!

Nowadays two famous systems are used.
Both are called after their inventors.
The older system is Labanotation, invented by Rudolf von Laban.
This is what it looks like:

The dance it records is *Funny Story* from Antony Tudor's
Little Improvisations.

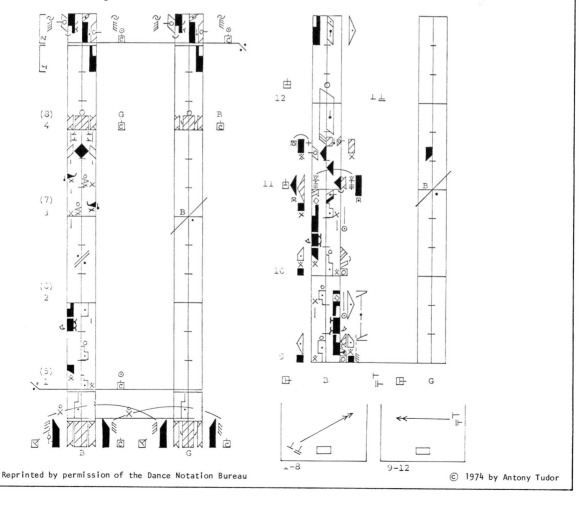

© 1974 by Antony Tudor

The other system is called Benesh notation, after its inventor, Rudolf Benesh. It looks like this:

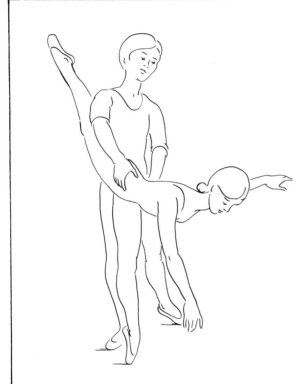

An example of Benesh notation showing four bars of the peasant pas de deux *from Act I of* GISELLE. *The girl does a* pas de bourrée *forward into a preparation in fourth position for a double turn, finishing in* attitude devant *supported by the boy (see illustration and area indicated by dotted line), then a* grand rond de jambe en l'air *into* arabesque *followed by* penchée *and* posé *into a* promenade in arabesque. *Music by Adam*

Institute of Choreology, London

The people who write down dances in Benesh notation are called choreologists.

*C*horeography *is only one* of the ingredients of a ballet. Music, costumes, and scenery also contribute. It is a union of many arts. All kinds of music are used by choreographers.

Andante Molto.

Sometimes a score is specially composed.
Sometimes a choreographer sets a ballet to other
forms of accompaniment—percussion rhythms or electronic
music, for instance.

For live music an orchestra is needed.
This photograph, taken from the wings, shows Robert Irving,
Music Director of New York City Ballet, conducting the
orchestra at the New York State Theater.

Costumes and scenery have always played an important part in
ballet.
The first costumes were based on the court dress of the period.
They were made of costly material and splendidly ornamented
with jewels and feathers.

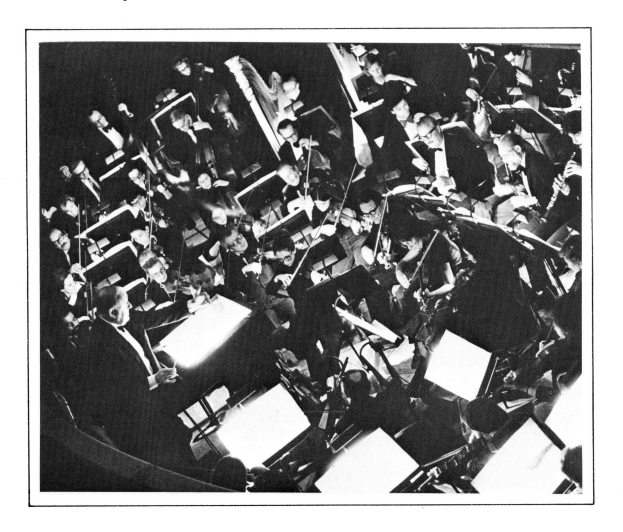

In the Romantic ballets costumes were much simpler.
The ballerinas wore what we now call a "romantic tutu."
"Tutu" is a French word for a ballet dress whose skirt is
made up of layers of net.
The romantic tutu has a full, calf-length skirt and a
tightly shaped bodice with a low neck and tiny cap sleeves
like the one worn by the Sylphide.
The romantic costume for a man consisted of tights and
a hip-length tunic, sometimes made of velvet.

This picture is of Eleanor d'Antuono, Karena Brock, and Ivan Nagy
of American Ballet Theatre, wearing romantic costume, in
Les Sylphides.

Les Sylphides is not the same ballet as *La Sylphide*.
It was choreographed very much later—the first version was
staged in 1906—by Mikhail Fokine in St. Petersburg.
The idea and style, however, were a tribute to the old Romantic
Period ballets.

When ballets like *The Sleeping Beauty, Swan Lake,* and *Don
Quixote* were produced, in the late nineteenth century, dancing
had developed a stage further. In the way that athletes are always
tackling more difficult feats, choreographers are always inventing
more difficult steps and dances. The ballerinas who created the
leading roles in Petipa's ballets needed shorter dresses to show
off the clever pirouettes and lifts he had choreographed for them.
So the dress we call the "classical tutu" came into fashion.
It is the familiar short, circular, stiffened skirt that you see
in this picture of Maria Calegari and Sean Lavery of New York City
Ballet, in George Balanchine's *Divertimento No. 15.*

Many other styles of costume are used nowadays. This photograph of Merrill Ashley of New York City Ballet in Balanchine's *Tchaikovsky Pas de Deux* shows a very popular type of dress with a draped skirt.

In many ballets the costumes are close-fitting "body tights" that show off the line of each position. Usually they have some slight decoration and a neat headdress. James Kudelka, Nadia Potts, and Miguel Garcia (L-R) of the National Ballet of Canada wear this kind of costume in Frederick Ashton's *Monotones II*.

Sometimes dancers have to wear very awkward costumes. In Balanchine's *A Midsummer Night's Dream*, which is based on

Shakespeare's play, Bottom the Weaver is magically
transformed by Puck into a donkey.
Here Laurence Matthews of New York City Ballet wears the
ass's head, as he partners Suzanne Farrell, who dances Titania.

The Royal Ballet dancers who took part in the film *The Tales of Beatrix Potter* were given an even more difficult task. They had to dance in costumes that made them look like the animal and bird characters from the illustrations in Beatrix Potter's famous children's stories.

In this picture Ann Howard is Jemima Puddle-Duck and Robert Mead is Mr. Fox.

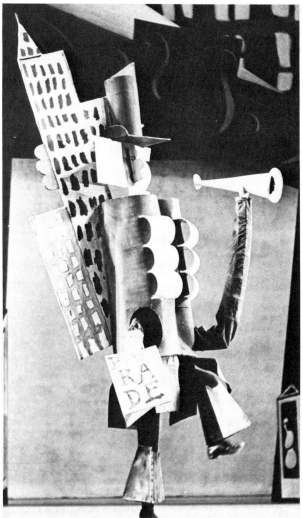

In Leonide Massine's ballet *Parade*, which is danced by the Joffrey Ballet and by London Festival Ballet, there are two Managers. One is French (*left*) and one is American. The extraordinary costumes were designed by the great painter Pablo Picasso. You will be able to work out for yourself where the heads of the dancers come, and how much the costume towers above them. The Managers do not, however, have to do very much dancing—unlike the characters in *The Tales of Beatrix Potter*.

*L*udmila *Vlasova* and Stanislav Vlasov, who appear with the Bolshoi Ballet, gave themselves an equally amazing task in an exciting *pas de deux*, *The Doves*, which they created. Each wears a stiffened "wing" covering one arm. The supported work, with high lifts like the spectacular one in this picture, has to be perfectly timed to avoid accidents.

When choreographers compose ballets, they draw on other kinds of dancing as well as on the technique of classical ballet. One of the most important is folk dancing.
There are folk dance traditions in every part of the world.

Sometimes a folk dance is used in a ballet very much as it would be performed by a folk dance company.
One of these is the mazurka in the first act of *Coppélia*, here led by Martine van Hamel and Michael Denard of American Ballet Theatre.

Sometimes, however,
folk dance steps are
mixed in with
classical ballet steps.

This picture might
easily be of a
men's folk dance
from Russia or
Yugoslavia.
In fact it is of
Helgi Tomasson and
Daniel Duell of
New York City Ballet
in Jerome Robbins's
*Dances at
a Gathering*.

Court dances of the past sometimes appear in ballets.
This one is danced in the hunting scene of the Royal Ballet's
production of *The Sleeping Beauty*.

Ballroom dances are
used as well.
Here is a comic
version of the tango,
from Frederick
Ashton's *Façade*,
danced by Ingrid
Fraley and Gary
Chryst of the
Joffrey Ballet.

Many ballets are based on the Viennese waltz and its variations. This picture shows dancers of New York City Ballet in Balanchine's *Vienna Waltzes*. Stage and film dancing of the Hollywood musical kind are used to good effect in ballet. Here Suzanne Farrell, Delia Peters, and Lisa de Ribere of New York City Ballet dance in Balanchine's *Union Jack*.

Dancers have to study all these kinds of dance—folk dance, historical dance, ballroom and stage dancing. They learn something about modern dance as well. The technique of modern dance is quite different from classical ballet. It is not based on the five positions of feet and arms, and the legs are not "turned out" from the hips as in classical ballet. It emphasizes what is called "floorwork." This means the movements dancers can make while they are lying or sitting on the floor. Classical ballet and modern dance used to be completely separate. Now, quite often, a modern dance choreographer will compose a ballet for a classical ballet company. Modern dancer and choreographer Twyla Tharp, seen here conducting a rehearsal, composed *Push Comes to Shove* for American Ballet Theatre.

Classical ballet choreographers also use many modern dance
steps in their ballets.
So ballet dancers sometimes work with modern dance teachers.

Other subjects are studied by dancers.
They learn music, art history, stage design, make-up.
They learn something of the
martial arts—kung-fu, perhaps, and fencing. Some ballets—
Romeo and Juliet, for instance—feature sword fights
specially arranged by an expert in stage dueling.

Ballet often uses positions from the gymnast's or acrobat's
repertoire. Here Gelsey Kirkland of American Ballet Theatre
limbers up very much as might an acrobat.

Another acrobatic position, this time onstage, by Irina Kolpakova as Eve in the Kirov Ballet's production *The Creation of the World*.

A high lift with an acrobatic look.
Alla Osipenko and John Markovsky are rehearsing for the Kirov Ballet's *The Stone Flower*.

If ballet borrows from gymnastics and acrobatics, various sports borrow from ballet. Ice skating is one of these. Ice skaters are more and more indebted to ballet training and good choreography. One of the pioneers was British John Curry, Olympic gold medalist. Here he performs an *arabesque* on skates.

Wearing a skate prevents a skater from having the cleancut line and pointed foot that marks the good ballet dancer. On the other hand, skaters can travel smoothly over the ice while they hold an *arabesque* or *attitude*. Curry now directs and tours with an "ice-dancing" group that is bringing skating and ballet very close together.

Soviet ice skaters adapt the supported work of classical ballet techniques for their pair skating programs. Here are international champions Irina Rodnina and Alexander Zaitsev.

ymnastic floorwork shares many elements with ballet. The word "floorwork" here means something different from its use in modern dance. It means the routine performed on the floor as opposed to work on bars or rings. A gymnast's floor performance resembles a dance when it is done by a skilled competitor like Irina Deryugina of the USSR.

Soccer is one of the less likely sports to have any association with ballet. Both, however, need good physical coordination and flexibility. They need skillful timing and neat footwork. The soccer players

in these pictures are trying to benefit from a ballet
class, but they are unlikely to rival Mikhail Baryshnikov!

What kind of life do ballet dancers lead? They begin to dance when they are very young. Their training gets more intensive as they grow older. They dance in student performances at school and join their first company when they are in their late teens. They learn to feel at home onstage. There is excitement in performing in a theater rather than in a studio. With a company, they begin to find out what it is like to dance for an audience. Audiences are as different as individual people in what they like and dislike. Some enjoy a long traditional work like *Swan Lake*. Some prefer programs of shorter, modern ballets. The way an audience reacts matters a great deal to a dancer. Just as an enthusiastic crowd can help an athlete to do well in a track event, an enthusiastic audience can encourage a dancer to give a fine performance. Ballet companies appear in opera houses,

in school halls, or before enormous audiences in the open air.
This picture shows the Boston Ballet at Hatch Shell on
the Boston Esplanade.

To begin with, dancers are in the *corps de ballet*. They dance
in the crowd in ballets like *The Sleeping Beauty* and *The Nutcracker*.
Then they are picked out to dance in a *pas de trois* or a *pas de
quatre* (dance for four). Later, they get a small solo role or
pas de deux. Later still, they dance, and perhaps create,
a leading role. Balletgoers begin to notice them. Ballet critics
begin to mention them. Their pictures appear in the dance magazines.
Someone asks for their autograph. Someone sends them flowers.
But the hard work never stops. A great deal depends on their work
at class and rehearsal. All the time they have to try and improve
their jumps, their pirouettes, their supported work. They have
to increase their strength and stamina. They have to memorize
many roles in new ballets. If they memorize leading roles as well
as the ones they are actually performing, they may become
understudies. Then they might have a chance to take over a role
if someone is sick. They have to try and do what choreographers
ask them to do, even if it is very difficult. They fall many
times as they rehearse. Sometimes they injure themselves.
They get strains, and sprains, and stress fractures of bones.
They have trouble with tendons and muscles and cartilage. Then
they have to consult physiotherapists and specialists.

A ballet company is a community. Dancers see a lot of each
other, at class, at meals in cafeterias, before, during and
after performances, and when they are traveling. They are among
the most widely traveled people in the world. Dancing is an
international language, and dancers are always on the move.

Even in the early years of this century the Russian ballerina
Anna Pavlova toured constantly. She did it by ship and train.
With her company she crossed North America, visited the Far East,
Australia and India, more than once. She brought ballet to
countless people who had never seen it before. Nowadays companies
travel by air. In this picture London Festival Ballet's dancers
are embarking in England for a tour of Australia.

Wherever dancers go, daily "company class" is vital to their work.
In the picture at the top of the next page a Soviet ballet master,
Asaf Messerer, takes company class with Australian Ballet dancers
Michela Kirkaldie, Valmai Roberts, Chrisa Keramidas, and
Hilary Debden.

Before a performance a company often has an onstage rehearsal.
The bottom picture shows London Festival Ballet dancers in
practice clothes of tights and T-shirts rehearsing for
Harald Lander's *Etudes*.

Etudes is a ballet *about* rehearsing and classwork. It begins with limbering and *barre* work, as this picture, taken during a performance by Paris Opera Ballet, makes clear.

The starriest stars of ballet travel most of their time. They appear internationally as guest artists, often in popular showpieces. This photograph is of Dame Margot Fonteyn and Rudolf Nureyev in the *pas de deux* from *Le Corsaire* (The Corsair).

Here are Natalia Makarova and Mikhail Baryshnikov in the *pas de deux* from *Don Quixote*.

Dancers appear in films and on television.
American Ballet Theatre dancers took part in the Twentieth
Century-Fox film *The Turning Point*.

These pictures show the cameramen filming them in *Etudes*.
and this is how they looked to the movie audience when
the film was released.

Dancers, in spite of work and dedication, do have lives and
hobbies outside the world of ballet.
Horseback riding and show-jumping are a passion with
Donald MacLeary of the Royal Ballet.

Margaret Barbieri
of the Sadler's
Wells Royal
Ballet is
a sparetime
gardener.

Dancers have
families.
They have
husbands and
wives and
children.
Often they
marry other
dancers.
Here Alain
Dubreuil of the
Sadler's Wells
Royal Ballet,
whose wife is
dancer Gillian
Shane, tries
out a cooking
recipe with
their son
Christian.

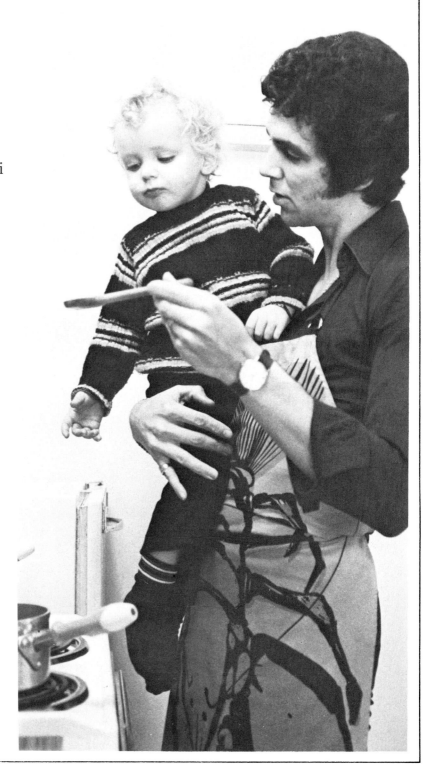

M̲ost dancers' children learn dancing.
It is a good thing for anyone to do, even if they are
not thinking of making it a career.
It helps them to carry themselves well.
It gives them more physical control, so that they
feel more confident and assured, as shown by these two
young students at the School of American Ballet.

There is pleasure to be had both from dancing and from watching dancing— the kind of enjoyment shown by young Tania as she watches her parents, Irina Kolpakova and Vladilen Semeonov of the Kirov Ballet, practicing a high lift in their garden.

SOME OTHER BOOKS ABOUT BALLET FOR YOU TO READ

GODDEN, RUMER, *The Tale of the Tales: The Beatrix Potter Ballet*

HARRIS, LEON, *Russian Ballet School*

KREMENTZ, JILL, *A Very Young Dancer*

LAWSON, JOAN, *The Story of Ballet*

STREATFEILD, NOEL, *A Young Person's Guide to Ballet*

SWOPE, MARTHA, *The Nutcracker*

UNTERMEYER, LOUIS, *Tales from the Ballet*

Index

5 6/13 Ln 2/13 5, circ wd lib